G000295371

Improve your sight-reading!

Paul Harris

Extra Stage: Revision available to download from
fabermusicstore.com

For online audio of all the pieces scan the QR code
or go to fabermusic.com/content/audio

FABER *ff* MUSIC

Practice chart

	Comments (from you, your teacher or parent)	Done!
Stage 1		
Stage 2		
Stage 3		
Stage 4		
Stage 5		

Teacher's name _____

Telephone _____

With many thanks to Gillian Secret for her invaluable help.

© 2011 by Faber Music Ltd
This edition first published in 2011 by Faber Music Ltd.
Bloomsbury House, 74–77 Great Russell Street, London WC1B 3DA
Music processed by Donald Thomson
Cover and page design by Susan Clarke
Printed in England by Caligraving Ltd

ISBN10: 0-571-53622-0
EAN13: 978-0-571-53622-1

US edition:
ISBN10: 0-571-53662-X
EAN13: 978-0-571-53662-7

To buy Faber Music publications or to find out about the full range of titles available
please contact your local music retailer or Faber Music sales enquiries:
Faber Music Ltd, Burnt Mill, Elizabeth Way, Harlow CM20 2HX
Tel: +44 (0) 1279 82 89 82   Fax: +44 (0) 1279 82 89 83
sales@fabermusic.com   fabermusicstore.com

Introduction

Being a good sight-reader is so important and it's not difficult at all!
If you work through this book carefully – always making sure that you
really understand each exercise before you play it – you'll never have
problems learning new pieces or doing well at sight-reading in exams!

Using the workbook

1 Rhythmic exercises

Make sure you have grasped these fully before you go on to the melodic
exercises: it is vital that you really know how the rhythms work. There
are a number of ways to do the exercises – see *Improve your sight-reading*
Grade/Level 1 for more details.

2 Melodic exercises

These exercises use just the notes (and rhythms) for the Stage, and are
organised into Sets which progress gradually. If you want to sight-read
fluently and accurately, get into the simple habit of working through
each exercise in the following ways before you begin to play it:

- Make sure you understand the rhythm and counting. Clap the
  exercise through.
- Know what notes you are going to play and the fingering you are
  going to use.
- Try to hear the piece through in your head. Always play the first
  note to help.

3 Prepared pieces

Work your way through the questions first, as these will help you to think
about or 'prepare' the piece. Don't begin playing until you are pretty sure
you know exactly how the piece goes.

4 Going solo!

It is now up to you to discover the clues in this series of practice pieces.
Give yourself about a minute and do your best to understand the piece
before you play. Check the rhythms and hand position, and try to hear
the piece in your head. Always remember to feel the pulse and to keep
going steadily once you've begun.

The **online audio** is for you to listen to *after* you have performed any
sight-reading piece. Use it to check whether you have understood the
rhythm and overall feel and style of the piece correctly.

Good luck and happy sight-reading!

Terminology:
Bar = measure

Stage 1

D and A major
2-note slurs

Rhythmic exercises

5 Make up your own rhythmic exercise:

Melodic exercises

Set 1: Introducing 2-note slurs

Set 2: Exercises with more movement

Set 3: Exploring slurs with string-crossings

Prepared pieces

1 What will you count? Tap the pulse and hear the rhythm in your head.

2 What is the key? Play the scale and arpeggio in a dancing style.

3 Can you spot any repeated patterns – rhythmic or melodic?

4 What is the interval between the first two notes called? Play the first note and sing the second. To which pattern do both notes belong?

5 How will you put some character into your performance?

1 How will you count this piece? Hear the pulse in your head and tap the rhythm.

2 In which key is the piece? Play the scale and arpeggio in a singing style.

3 The first two notes belong to the arpeggio – how many more examples can you find of two-note patterns that belong to the arpeggio?

4 How many bars share the same rhythm as bar 1? How is bar 3 similar to bar 1?

5 How will you put character into your performance?

Improvising

Make up your own piece (it can be as long or as short as you like), beginning with this pattern. Keep the pulse steady. Decide on a mood or character before you begin.

Now make up your own piece in A major – using any patterns you like.

Going solo!

Don't forget to prepare each piece carefully before you play it.

Stage 2

G major

Rhythmic exercises

Always remember to count two bars in.

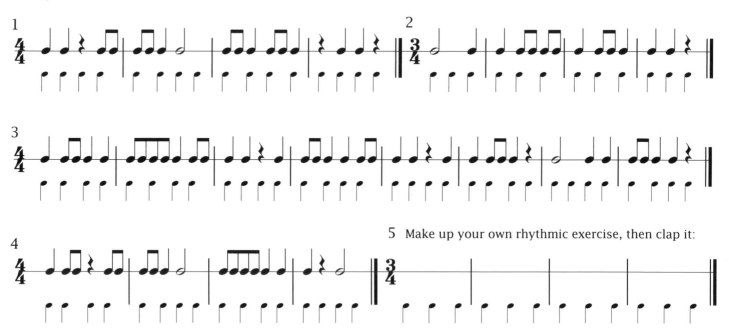

5 Make up your own rhythmic exercise, then clap it:

Melodic exercises

Set 1: Exploring C natural on the A string

Set 2: Exploring the upper notes

Set 3: Exploring the full octave

Set 4: Exploring the lower octave

Prepared pieces

1 What is the key of this piece? Play the scale and arpeggio expressively.

2 Can you spot any repeated patterns – rhythmic or melodic? Are there any scale or arpeggio patterns?

3 What is the interval formed by the last note in bar 2 and first note of bar 3? How will you finger it? Does the same interval occur again?

4 What will you count? Tap the pulse and think through the rhythm, then tap the rhythm and think the pulse.

5 How will you put some character into your performance?

1

1 Play the scale of this piece sturdily.

2 What is similar about bars 1 and 2? Are there any more similar bars?

3 Count in your head and tap the rhythm.

4 Play the first note and try to hear the piece in your head.

5 What gives you clues to the character of this piece?

2

Improvising

1

Make up your own piece (it can be as long or as short as you like), beginning with this pattern. Keep the pulse steady. Decide on a mood or character before you begin.

2

Now make up your own piece in G major, using any patterns you like.

Going solo!

Don't forget to prepare each piece carefully before you play it.

Stage 3

E (natural)
minor

Rhythmic exercises

Always remember to count two bars in.

5 Make up your own rhythmic exercise, then clap it:

Melodic exercises

Set 1: Introducing E (natural) minor

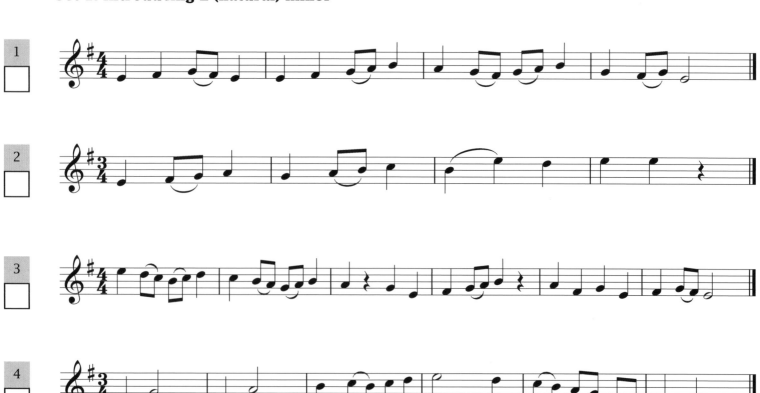

Set 2: Exploring thirds

Set 3: Exploring fourths

Set 4: Mixed intervals

Prepared pieces

1 What is the key of this piece? Play the scale and arpeggio.

2 Which notes are affected by the key signature?

3 Can you spot any repeated patterns – rhythmic or melodic? Are there any scale patterns?

4 What will you count? Tap the pulse and think the rhythm through, then tap the rhythm and think the pulse.

5 How will you put character into your performance?

1 What is the interval formed by the first two notes? Play the notes. Is there another example of this interval?

2 What is similar about bars 1 and 2? Are there any more similar bars?

3 Tap the pulse with your foot and the rhythm with your hands.

4 Play the first note and then try to hear the piece in your head.

5 How will you put some character into your performance?

Improvising

Make up your own piece (it can be as long or as short as you like), beginning with this pattern. Keep the pulse steady. Decide on a mood or character before you begin.

Now make up your own piece in E minor – using any notes of the scale you like.

Going solo!

Don't forget to prepare each piece carefully before you play it.

Stage 4

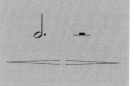

Rhythmic exercises

Always remember to count two bars in.

5 Make up your own rhythmic exercise, then clap it:

Melodic exercises

Set 1: Exploring ♩.

Set 2: Exploring –

Set 3: Exploring more arpeggio patterns

Set 4: More ♩. and –

Prepared pieces

1 What is the key of this piece? Play the scale and arpeggio flowingly.

2 Can you spot any repeated patterns – rhythmic or melodic? Are there any scale or arpeggio patterns?

3 Study the last two bars for a few moments then play them from memory.

4 What will you count? Tap the pulse and think through the rhythm, then think the pulse and tap the rhythm.

5 How will you put some character into your performance?

1

1 Think through the bowing in your head.

2 Can you find any notes that belong to the arpeggio of G major?

3 Count the pulse in your head and tap the rhythm.

4 Play the first note and try to hear the piece in your head.

5 What gives you a clue to the character of the piece?

2

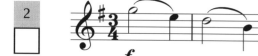

Improvising

1

Make up your own piece (it can be as long or as short as you like), beginning with this pattern. Keep the pulse steady. Decide on a mood or character before you begin.

2

Now make up your own piece – include some longer notes and rests.

Going solo!

Don't forget to prepare each piece carefully before you play it.

Stage 5

Rhythmic exercises

Always count two bars before you begin each exercise – one aloud and the second silently.

5 Make up your own rhythmic exercise, then clap it:

Sight-reading confidently

Read the words in this box:

Here are some words in a box which I am reading correctly.

No problem! You looked at the words, said them (to yourself) *and* understood what they meant! It's the same with music. As long as you know the rhythms and know the notes, playing them is just the same as reading words. If you can do all the rhythmic exercises in this book (easily and on your own) and you know the notes of the four keys we've been working through (D, A and G majors and E minor) then you should be able to sight-read confidently.

Look at this next piece for a few moments. Read it like you're reading these words. Hear it in your head, then read on…

Moderato

Did you 'understand' it? Do you 'get' what it's about? Do you feel you have a good idea of how it goes?

… You know it's in D major and you can see all the scale patterns and you know how you'll finger the piece. You know all the rhythms, you understand the bowing. So you should feel confident about playing it. Have a go.

Your performance was almost certainly accurate, strong and... confident!

Now let's try that again with this piece. Look at it and work out what it's saying:

1

Do you feel you've got it? The key, the notes, the rhythms – and did you notice the important word at the start? **'Boldly'**. Now do just that – play it accurately, confidently and boldly!

Do the same with the next pieces. Get into the habit of being really confident about your sight-reading.

Prepared pieces

> **1** What is the key of this piece? Play the scale and arpeggio like a fanfare.
>
> **2** How many times does the rhythm pattern in bar 1 return?
>
> **3** To what pattern do all the notes in the first two bars belong? Play the pattern.
>
> **4** Read through the piece, hearing it in your head.
>
> **5** What is the character of the music? How will you put that character into your performance?

1

> **1** Think the bowing through in your head.
>
> **2** Have a quick look through the piece. Do you feel you understand it?
>
> **3** Count in your head and tap the rhythm.
>
> **4** Play the first note and hear the piece in your head.
>
> **5** What are the clues to the character of this piece?

2

Improvising

1

> Make up your own piece (it can be as long or as short as you like), beginning with this pattern. Keep the pulse steady. Decide on a mood or character before you begin.
>
>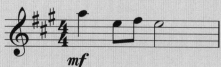
>
> Now make up your own piece – use any patterns you like.

2

Going solo!

Don't forget to prepare each piece carefully before you play it.

The golden rules

A sight-reading checklist

Before you begin to play a piece at sight, always consider the following:

1 Look at the piece for about half a minute and try to feel that you are *understanding* what you see (just like reading these words).

2 Look at the time signature and decide how you will count the piece.

3 Look at the key signature and think about how to finger the notes.

4 Notice patterns – especially those that repeat, or are based on scales and arpeggios.

5 Notice any markings that will help you convey the character.

6 Don't begin until you think you are going to play the piece accurately.

7 Count at least one bar in.

When performing a sight-reading piece

1 Keep feeling the pulse.

2 Keep going at a steady tempo.

3 Remember the finger pattern of the key you are in.

4 Ignore mistakes.

5 Look ahead – at least to the next note.

6 Play musically, always trying to convey the character of the music.